## CONTENTS

Foreword

Introduction

Chapter 1: Dealing with Diabetes

Chapter 2: Having a Good Life

Chapter 3: Understanding Blood Sugar Levels

Chapter 4: Managing Type 1

Chapter 5: Life Experiences

Chapter 6: Mum and The Pitty Potty

Chapter 7: Life On The Pump

Chapter 8: Never Defeated

# FOREWORD

Jon-Sel Gourkan has an eclectic and captivating life story having had careers in professional sport, the music industry and as an actor. Over the course of his football career in Turkey he managed to win a similar award to what David Beckham had won at the Bobby Charlton Football School. In England Jon-Sel was looked after by Jerome Anderson when trying to gain a contract with Tony Pulis's Gillingham F.C. He had trials in Turkey and signed as a professional footballer with First Division Altay S.K and then went onto play for Galatasaray Under 21's. This all ended abruptly when he couldn't continue his career due to being a Type 1 Diabetic.

Jon-Sel then decided to go back to his routes in the entertainment industry attending drama school which then led to many opportunities. He pursued a path in the music industry and joined a pop act called Word On The Street (WOTS), which toured the U.K with 5ive, Westlife, Atomic Kitten, Bewitched and were nominated for Best New Tour Act on The Smash Hits Poll Winners Party Show. Jon-Sel went on to sign a solo deal, his first single 21$^{st}$ Century Man was used on Showtime's American version of Queer as Folk.

Jon-Sel's love of performing then took him back into acting. His many acting credits include Love's Labours Lost at the Royal Shakespeare Company and Karen Bruce's West End Hit Fame the Musical. Most recently his one man show Keep Calm I'm Only Diabetic has toured across the United Kingdom.

A special thank you to Jondon, Gail Rolfe, Ewa Gourkan, Mark Lockyer, John Mckie, Amanda Harris and all at Diabetes UK for their support throughout this process

# INTRODUCTION

I have been a Type 1 for 28 years, I have had problems, I have met idiots who can't deal with it, but I have had many who have stood by me when I have been close to falling over the edge. The world isn't against you, it can be just you beating yourself up for no apparent reason.

Diabetes, just what is it? A place that is so exotic, it makes the Caribbean seem second best when relating it to a luxurious surrounding? Or is it a beautiful foreign name that only the best looking people in the world have? We could go on saying diabetes is a beautiful word one falls in love with, but unfortunately it's something that can strike you at any time in your life. It's just an annoyance that is looked after through eating the right foods, keeping fit, looking after one's self, and taking the correct medication, and being clever enough to look after your body in a sensible way. I am sure some of you are saying, "YEAH, LIKE THAT'S ALL IT INVOLVES!" That is simply the truth of the matter, it's fact and definitely not fiction. There is no such word as can't, the words "YES I CAN DEAL WITH IT" will certainly take you to further fields with a smile on your face, and it will make a difference to the world.

Anything where hospitals, injections and long named illnesses are mentioned definitely scares us all. It is a shock to the system when being told you have to deal with something medically in your life, but like anything in life, you can overcome anything that is put in your way. When you're first told "I'M SORRY TO SAY THIS BUT YOU HAVE DIABETES" it makes you lose all your senses, you sweat in a nervous manner, and your face drops.

I suppose I was lucky to be diagnosed with diabetes at a very young age, rather than later on in life. I was only twelve but I knew what diabetes was, and what it meant in terms of dealing with it. My mum is a Type 1 and my grandfather was a Type 2, so it was something I had grown up with. Did I think OH NO? when I was told "YOUNG MAN YOU'RE A DIABETIC". I would be lying if I said I didn't. Diabetes was treated very differently when I was first diagnosed, and it is indeed looked at in a different way now. At the time I was first diagnosed it did mean no more junk food or sugary things, but I could live with that, as I hadn't been handed a death sentence. Diabetics are indeed superb human beings, and if we just take extra care of ourselves we will remain the best of the bunch. I have many experiences that I want to share with the hot to trot generation of diabetic youngsters, and even the diabetic oldies, making each and every one of you realize that it's not the end of the world; it is the beginning of all things big, bright, and beautiful. No one is perfect, perfection isn't possible, we can look for it but you have to remember that failure is trying to please everybody else. It is your life and you pull the strings, you make the choices and you choose how you want to live.

Not many people understand the word diabetes, people think it's eating sugar, injecting yourself, and that makes you feel on top of the world. KNOCK KNOCK? There is no answer, these kinds of people with I HAVE NO SENSE written across their forehead are not even worth worrying about. All that counts is you as a diabetic knowing how to handle certain situations, and to pass on your knowledge to those that don't understand what it's all about.

Young diabetics are just given leaflets and boring information to help them cope. It is a bit like Sunday afternoon television; it sends you to sleep and leaves you with a look that represents "WHY OH WHY IS THIS BEING PUT BEFORE MY VERY EYES?". I am not surprised that legendary young diabetic superstars are shocked by what they are told, as it is boring and not put from our point of view. Any old man professor or foul breathed doctor giving us diabetic information is never entertaining or interesting.

I just want today's generation of people to know that diabetes can be looked after you can lead a life of harmony and bliss, it is just a small problem as an organ in our body has broken down. Cars break down, you give a car fuel and it goes. Diabetics breakdown, sugar boosts us back up to our superstar way of thinking, High blood sugar makes an uninvited appearance, and we give ourselves a correction dose to snap us out of Dr. Jekyll and Mr. Hyde mode. Insulin is our fuel and that keeps us going on a twenty-four/seven basis.

On a daily basis no matter what, believe all is well, believe there is more to life, just smile, and never feel like the odd one out. Feel like the chosen one, the one who can teach others right and wrong about diabetes, and the one who won't be beaten. Diabetics are fighters and indeed superstars, we set the trends, so inject in public without a single care in the world. Let people stare, it is nothing to be ashamed of, it is something to be proud of. If people do stare, just say to yourself "I AM GREAT, AND I APPRECIATE ALL EYES BEING ON ME".

Remember to never be scared or be afraid. Diabetics are survivors, and you can be the biggest survivor if you just look after yourself, and give yourself time to realize that it really isn't the end of the world.

# CHAPTER ONE - DEALING WITH DIABETES

When it comes to dealing with your family and friends, (especially those who think they know absolutely everything regarding Type 1) diabetes can become a huge problem: "WHY ARE YOU EATING SUGAR? WHY ARE YOU INJECTING YOURSELF? SHOULDN'T YOU BE TAKING TABLETS?" Dealing with teachers at school, a jobsworth manager in a work environment, someone staring at you in a restaurant? You can get incredibly stupid remarks thrown your way when you simply imply that you are having a hypo, having a hyper, and you are in desperate need of a sugar boost. We can all make lame excuses, but the truth is, we can help ourselves by being honest. In life, we sometimes blame others for our mistakes, but it is all our own doing, and we are the ones that pull the strings when dealing with situations in everyday life.

I'm not saying that problems that occur in our lives are easy, but what exactly is easy in everyday life? Sitting on our behinds? Yes that is true, but it's boring. Diabetes isn't something to be scared of, in fact, it is probably scared of us. We the mighty human being can defeat anything. Why is a stupidly named health condition going to put us off maintaining our dreams and true goals in life? If we don't look after ourselves, then diabetes is only winning. No-one likes to be beaten, it's just as bad as a dreaded Xmas gift from an annoying relative, or a loved one making you wear a knitted skintight jumper on a hot summer's day. It certainly isn't nice, but we have to do it. The same goes for diabetes, it isn't nice but we have to deal with it.

I do realise that not everyone is positive with certain situations in life, but there is always a time to start. You must remember that there is no such word as CAN'T. You can look at diabetes as if it is a nasty bully who is always giving you grief. Bullies never win. WHY? Cause they are cowards. Diabetes is the same, it is bullying our body. CAN WE BEAT IT? For sure we can, its cowardly of us not to look after ourselves, but to beat any bully or obstacle in life, we have to stand up to it and confront it. So mighty fine gorgeous diabetics just HOW DO WE STAND UP TO IT? We inject our insulin, check our blood sugar levels at regular intervals, eat in a healthy manner, stay fit, and yes if we all stick to that, we become true geniuses by overhauling the criminal that is Type 1. Diabetics may as well call themselves superheroes; we are defending ourselves, and protecting others against the criminal who never comes out on top, MR DIABETIC PATHETIC. All criminals eventually get beaten at their own game, they never win. The Joker keeps plotting to outdo Batman but never succeeds, Dr Octopus always trying to outdo Spiderman but always losing out at the last minute, and the mighty Superman always stopping the evil Lex Luther from instigating a nasty crime. Look at diabetes in a way where you can see it as being weak, and not being able to break you down into small stages. If something is pathetic it never comes out on top, and like the underdog, we always rise to reach the status we deserve, and that status is that of a champion.

People never really understand how diabetes affects our everyday life. The thing is unless you have diabetes, you're not going to know how we feel when having a hypo. How agitated we get when having high blood sugar? At the end of the day, we aren't here to worry about what others think, we are here to look after ourselves, and to make sure we survive with what we have to deal with. I am a male, well at least I hope I am considering last time I checked I was, and I don't know how it feels when females have their ladylike problems. When you break a bone it is a nasty feeling and it is ever so painful, so unless you have had a broken bone you won't know what it feels like. This is the same as diabetes, we mend back together and pick ourselves up, and continue to live our everyday lives like every other person. Anyway being normal is so yesterday, Why be like everyone else? Crazy, insane, happy, wise, and clever, these kinds of traits I would rather have than being classed as one who is seen as being normal.

Clark Kent was normal, but his secret was that he was Superman, so not everything is what it seems. The same goes for all superheroes: Peter Parker - a normal everyday person who transformed into Spider-Man when people cried out for help, Bruce Wayne - the sophisticated polite gent who turned into the Dark Knight Batman when those in distress needed help. We need to help ourselves by taking our insulin, and doing the correct thing when eating certain foods. If we don't then like any criminal we are neglecting those who need help, and we can refer that to our pancreas as being the bystander who needs help. Our pancreas is in need of insulin to help survive everyday life. Just because you inject yourself, it doesn't mean that you are an outcast. Count it as being one who leads two lives, as its better to lead two lives as it enables you to have more get up and go and gives you electrifying intensity. Diabetics are definite superheroes, they protect the diabetic community serving those on the outside, with the correct knowledge to understand.

We all handle things in different ways, I don't expect people to have the same attitudes as me, but I really want all diabetics to know that they are not alone. We are growing in force, and by us all sticking together, we will be a force to be reckoned with. It's all about focusing our minds on the positive things in life, rather than the negative. Never lose focus, and remember you can always change your way of thinking, from that of negative to that of a positive.

I want everyone to believe that diabetics are not different from anybody else, we all have the same coloured blood and breathe in the same air. Deal with any problem you have in your own respectable way. This doesn't mean that you can't chase your dreams and reach the goals that you have set out in front of you. A saying which I swear by is WHAT'S THE POINT OF HAVING DREAMS IF YOU'RE NOT GOING TO MAKE THEM HAPPEN? Standing tall and smiling is enough to make you put that front foot forward, and to go head-on into any situation, with you coming out raising your hands, shouting out VICTORY. Do not ever think you are beaten, remember people are here to support and to get you on the right track. The hospital or even your doctor is there to help get you on track, so if any problems arise go straight to those in the know and talk about what's bugging you. Any problem that is kept hidden within just builds, and ends up developing from something so small into something as high as Simon Cowell's ridiculous hairdo, which does enough damage to a comb let alone your eyesight. It is good to talk, and once you set yourself on the right path, you will also be able to help those who have dealt with situations you have also encountered before.

Never be afraid, and never think it's a battle you are fighting on your own. There are times when I feel it is me against the world, but this is just my frustration coming out, and trying to pin the blame on others for my problems. I will always say this: raise your head up high and believe that nothing can stand in the way of you living an ordinary life, which I'm 100 percent sure will work out to be the most spectacular life you could have ever wished for. Live life in colour and high definition, and just see what you attract. Hypos will be in fear, and a normal blood sugar level of 6.0 will become your new best friend, that will surely give you the edge to take the world by storm.

It's always easier said than done when it comes to those giving advice about diabetes when they really have no idea how we feel on the inside? People will always say the classic lines of: "Diabetes is because you have too much sugar in your system."Oh, diabetes is because you can eat loads of sugar as you don't want to feel weak.!" Diabetes isn't talked about, as people will presume that everyone knows about it, and understands it. Epilepsy and asthma I'm sure are treated exactly the same. It will wind you up that various people think they are medical experts giving out the greatest advice. I used to get incredibly fed up with the way everyone thought they understood what diabetes is and how a diabetic should treat their body. It isn't their fault that they have no idea, it's up to us to not feel the fear, to be proud, and to just tell people exactly how diabetes works.

You deal with any experience you have in life the best way possible. You have to live your life the way you want to and deal with the consequences if you do indeed take a wrong turning. Remember that whenever you take a wrong turn it is easy to get back on the right track and head in the direction you had originally set out to follow. The worst thing you can do is make excuses, excuses don't cut it in the real world, and the only person you are letting down is yourself if you decide to keep avoiding all the truthful factors.

Joey Essex uses his hairspray like a diabetic should test their blood sugar on a regular basis, the females in the Only Way Is Essex use hair dye like a diabetic should be exercising on a regular basis, and the judges on reality TV programmes are like an overload of junk food which a diabetic should stay away from indefinitely. Relate your diabetes to people you can relate to and handle it in a way that keeps you afloat, being able to progress without a care in the world. Think big, dream big, and without your health you have no wealth, so put things in a bigger perspective as material things mean nothing.

We always think that we are invincible, and nothing can stop us or hold us back. The problem is with health-related issues we may not feel we are causing any damage at this moment in time, but in the long term we are setting ourselves up for a massive fall from a great height. My mum is a perfect example of this, and she has plenty of regrets later on in her life where she is saying "Oh if only I had looked after myself. If only I had paid more attention to the doctors. I should have just listened, rather than presume I had better knowledge than those who were dishing out the advice". Doctors can bore you, and they can be like reading a book which seems to go nowhere, but if you just stick to reading that book you will end up with knowledge that was unexpected but works out in your favour in the long-run. The boring voices of some doctors sound so repetitive, and we all have a quiet word with ourselves saying OH WILL YOU JUST SHUT UP, YEAH YEAH YEAH LIKE YOU UNDERSTAND YOU FOOL. The thing is they do understand, but they just don't have a way of getting these points across in a manner in which we want to hear them. You are not alone in thinking this; all diabetics will at some point reach the point of no-return where SHUT UP just becomes a word which you want to use on a regular basis. My mum never listened to those boring doctors, but they were always 110 per cent right; she has struggled later on in life with her Type 1 having had a heart attack, a toe amputation, and getting cardiovascular disease. This is all because she didn't care about herself and took too many things for granted, thinking diabetes wouldn't get the better of her. Things happen, and we would all like to turn back the clock at some point in our life, but this is impossible yet beating diabetes is possible. It's all about getting that strength and trying your best to lead the very best life you can lead. Bad blood sugars will happen, you have to remember every day is a new day that can bring something new your way, and in our case, it's a good blood sugar reading minus the temper tantrums we can throw when we have high or low blood sugar. It's no one's duty to understand, it's our own duty to understand, and if we have any problems we ask those close to us for advice, our diabetic consultant's, and even those doctors you just want to slap around the face with a wet fish.

The best thing is that there are plenty of diabetic discussion forums online along with diabetic chat rooms. The support is out there, and fellow diabetics are always on hand to help in your times of need. If you were the only person with diabetes in the world then I would understand how hard it would be, but you're not, and the problems you face others are also facing. I know some people find it hard to talk about their problems and issues with diabetes, but the moment you make the effort to try and open up, I can guarantee you that life will get that little bit better. Make it your mission to be proud, and to stand up for what you believe in, helping others who are also finding it hard. Everything takes time, and it's all a matter of pushing yourself to reach your very best, and not what others feel is your best. Opinions of those that don't understand don't count, as they are just like sheep following everyone else, thinking they are qualified doctors with a diagnosis for sorting out our lifestyle and dietary plans.

Things will get better and I just want you to remember that when a bad day happens you just need to sit down, take a deep breath and tell yourself "Tomorrow is a new day, and today I have just learnt how to handle things which haven't gone my way". You are the king or queen of your own world, and like the first man on the moon, you can plant your flag anywhere you like shouting out "I'M DIABETIC, AND I DON'T SWEAT THE SMALL STUFF". The icing on the cake is to smile so big that people think 'I need some of what they are having!'

# CHAPTER TWO - HAVING A GOOD LIFE

Life is what we make of it, and it is indeed a beautiful thing. Not everything goes according to plan, but in the long run, the good always outweighs the bad. It's just a matter of sailing through those torrid storms, to come out smiling at our dream destination. Diabetes is a mystery to many people, there are many mysteries in life, and some are yet to be discovered. There will always be several people who class themselves as know it alls, and who could crack the weakest link with ease, but people of this calibre are just putting on a show. Not everyone knows the full facts of life, and that's classed along with the same lines as outsiders thinking they have the ultimate knowledge of Type 1 diabetes.

It is never good to be told you have to diet and watch what you have to eat. No one likes to be told what to do. When your wife, girlfriend, boyfriend or parents tell you to tidy the house, clean the car, entertain the unwanted dinner guest, and wash the plates, it does echo the words HELL NO. If we do the things we are told we have to do, then usually there are no problems and the conversation can be moved forward onto something which is that of interesting nature. Looking after yourself when Type 1 is concerned is a valuable and a very important thing. We want to live life to the fullest, and the only way we can do that is to pay attention to the rules, and this, in the long run, will enable us to lead an adventurous life. It is easier said than it is easier done; we can all make sacrifices, but not many of us stick to them for a certain amount of time. We will break rules in life, even so called jobsworths break the rules. People who are put in high-class job roles, or have jobs where they are able to lead with a title have been known to lie. Not everything is straightforward and as clean cut as it seems. All these things we can relate to looking after ourselves with diabetes. Bad days will happen, and we will have a fine selection of doughnuts, cans of Coke, and eat junk food in a Homer Simpson fashion. We sometimes forget to cover ourselves with the correct amount of insulin after having a binge, but what's been done cannot be undone, so the important thing is to just learn from the tiny mistake we may have made. When it is bad, there can be only good, and vice-versa. You have a bad day, and from this, you have to tell yourself to move forward in a positive way, and not back into a pit of despair. Don't ever dwell on the bad day you had, as this won't put you in the right frame of mind to gain a positive attitude to move forward. I never thought to myself that it was the end of the world when I was diagnosed with Type 1. Life is short, and it is sweet, so if I couldn't have sweets, I would indeed enjoy life to the fullest, adding sweetness to other departments of my life. When I was first diagnosed the medication wasn't as advanced, and the dieticians were against any sugar being eaten at all. We step forward 25 years and it has all changed. The perception, and how one should live with diabetes has also changed. It shows us that things are being done, people are learning more, and changes are indeed inevitable. Always look for a positive way out of a tricky situation, negative thoughts only bring you down, and never bring you out on top.

Type 1 can't, and won't stop you doing what you want to do. People might tell you different but it's all a myth. Times have changed, more people are becoming diabetic, so it is only fair that everything is looked at in a professional way. Most jobs any diabetic can do, it just depends on what the job role entails. If you want to be a professional sportsperson, world famous actor/actress, entertainer, television spokesperson, lawyer, then this can be done. The unlucky people who don't really understand diabetes can't tell you that diabetics are only suited to certain jobs in life. I was told once that a diabetic couldn't work in a bakery as they would eat all the sugar, and my response to this was to never have this person involved in a Trivial Pursuits competition. Those who make comments like that should be seen, not heard, and just laughed at. Type 1's can eat what they want, it is just a matter of giving us the correct amount of insulin to cover us, and to jolt us back to our Hollywood superstar status. Ignore ignorant comments, and look at it as if that person is making a very bad joke. I have learnt never to make comments or make the judgement on things I don't understand. So people who think diabetics should be hyperactive when having a hypo or diabetics need a special badge on their forehead, they should do their homework, and learn that stupidity does nothing for their self-esteem.

I have done many things in life that have involved being in the public eye, and when mentioning that I have diabetes they all look at me like I'M SPECIAL. Well, I didn't want to disappoint them, as diabetics are individuals with elegant individual style. From a very early age I had always wanted to be the centre of attention, the one who made people laugh and entertained in a ridiculous madcap way. Just because I was diagnosed with diabetes wasn't going to put a stop to my madness, in fact, it was probably going to make me more resilient, and give me the knowledge to pass on to others that being different in whatever way it may seem, isn't a problem at all. My main love was football, to me football was life and it was something I couldn't live without. I can't live without my insulin, so I will take as much care to remember to take my medication, as I took care of watching my beloved football teams Galatasaray and

Queens Park Rangers play. Try and relate things that you love to your diabetes, if you ever miss out on the things you love in life, you get upset and annoyed. Your pancreas will get annoyed, and upset if you don't feed it insulin, so try and associate certain situations with you remembering to look after yourself.

I had a hard 8 years where I gave up on myself a little bit. I wasn't testing my blood and thought I could guess my blood sugar readings, so I would give myself the wrong dose of my Novorapid along with my evening dose of Lantus. This was dangerous and extremely stupid. It will happen when you have tough times, but I have learnt the hard way, and been very close to going into a diabetic coma as I've had bad hypos, yet I've been lucky enough to have an amazing dad and understanding friends who have been my saving grace, and saved the day. I don't want any diabetic to suffer from this, and the scary thing is that yes, you can die if you're not aware enough of what is going on. Tough words can scare anyone, but the simple truth is you have to be that little bit sharper than everyone else. So you're no good at maths or another subject which really sends you to sleep, but be the most educated person about yourself, and give yourself amazing top grades by being the most intelligent person about that annoying thing called diabetes which tries to knock your door down, but never succeeds. You may think that a person in your class or in life is much cleverer than you, but this isn't the case. You know more about diabetes, and they haven't got a clue. You have more chance of being a diabetic consultant with a supreme understanding, yet those who are the chiefs in lacking brain cells just know facts which are irrelevant to how you live your life. It's not important. What is important is you knowing your body, and knowing how to look after it, giving you a life which puts your name up in bright lights.

# CHAPTER 3 - UNDERSTANDING BLOOD SUGAR LEVELS

The hypos I have had which have been extremely bad have been a learning experience, and like anything which takes an effect on your life, you indeed learn from your mistakes. They need to be corrected, and you have to be adult enough to admit fault, moving on in a positive way by knowing where you went wrong previously. Sometimes it is recommended that you have a glass of milk, some digestives and a banana. This seems like the correct thing to do when you're first diagnosed, and I bit my tongue when I was told that this was what you needed to eat when having a hypo. It seemed that no matter how much distress you felt, and how weak you felt inside, you would need to prepare a Mary Poppins picnic in order to get a normal feeling back in your body. For a start I hate digestives, I find them to be old peoples biscuits, and I am not ready to move into an old people's home just yet to talk about walking up a mountain with Dr Doolittle and having a dodgy biscuit to give me energy. Bananas are great, yet they do tend to send my blood sugars through the roof, but they are a good source of energy, and they get me out of shaking at the knees ready to address a panel of judges in a ballroom, so that isn't too bad. Milk is also ok, but when drinking it I feel like I'm back at school being shoved into a corner to drink my carton of milk like a naughty little boy. I somehow didn't feel I would stick to the teddy bears picnic hypo meal, and I didn't. The doctors also recommended that having glucose tablets would help the effects of a hypo; they indeed would but they felt like I was eating chalk. The recommended dose was a couple, but when having a hypo you get the biggest hunger, and if the Titanic ship was a large burger you would indeed eat it in a matter of seconds. I don't think a magician of Dynamo's talent could make a piece of food disappear as quickly as we could make food vanish when having a hypo. Diabetics I am proud to say make pregnant women with their food cravings seem timid when going through the hypo syndrome.

I remember when I was at school a few weeks after I had been let out of the hospital with diabetes, I was carrying around a small Teenage Mutant Ninja Turtle tin with glucose tablets in it. The words Yummy Yummy didn't spring to mind. I tried to stick to the doctor's advice of taking a couple of glucose tablets, but it didn't happen, I started munching a lot of food at rapid speed. My hunger was more ferocious than a lion in the wild, I could have been classed as my school's NO STRANGER TO THE TUCK SHOP. Having a hypo does mean you need sugar to get your blood sugar level back to normal again, but if you go over the top with your sugar intake then you end up having blood sugar that is all over the shop. High blood sugar also leaves us feeling irritated, and gives us a very harsh thirst, sometimes taking us back to the way we felt before we were diagnosed with having diabetes. This is why it is extremely important to not overdo it when treating our hypos. If we do go too far with what we have just eaten, then it's having to be sensible by testing our blood sugar and then giving ourselves a correction dose. We will at some point do this, we can't always be saintly, and pay attention to the rules, but in the long run, we will feel a lot better for treating hypos in the correct manner.

When we have hypos in the middle of the night, this can be horrible. I sometimes feel that a hypo is just part of my dream, and the feeling will go away, but you eventually realise that it's actually happening, and the sweat dripping onto your bed sheets isn't because of the central heating, but a warning sign telling us that we have low blood sugar, and it needs to be treated straight away. I always look classy when having a hypo in the middle of the night, hair standing up on end resembling a creature from the cantina in Star Wars, sweat dripping off my forehead like I've been sitting in a sauna, and a lovely bit of sleepy dribble hanging out of the side of my mouth. This is why having bad hypos are not such a good look. So I recommend that testing your blood and seeing where you are at before you go to sleep is essential. Remember - waking up and looking like a zombie can cause whoever you live with a lot of pain as they have always imagined you to be the perfect picture. Well, I've got news for you, diabetics have a good reason for looking a bit shaky at times, it's part of the process, plus it shows another side to the glamorous way we live our lives.


Always remember to carry a sugar supply with you wherever you go. If you go on a journey, suddenly have a bad hypo, and you're without sugar you are in deep trouble. It might be annoying to carry around a Mars bar, a can of Monster, or Gluco tabs, but it's so important. There have been many times when I have had a hypo and been without sugar, but I had to hold on until I reached a shop that sold what I needed. If a hypo reaches a critical stage, you start to chat gibberish and you can come across as drunk, plus people won't take you seriously especially if they don't know that you're a diabetic. I remember I had entered a tennis tournament as a youngster and when walking home I suddenly when into a deep hypo stage. I hadn't taken any caution before I played, and I didn't check my blood sugar either, so I didn't really know where I was at. I can count it as being lazy, but you haven't got time to be lazy, you always have to be on top of the game or otherwise you can end up being in a really bad situation. I had to walk into a leisure centre looking like Krusty the Clown going through the bad hypo stage, and luckily I had enough normality left to get a chocolate bar and several other sugar supplements. People did stop and stare as I was shouting things and wandering around like an underage drunk. I do like to entertain, but looking like a sweaty drunk at the age of 14 doesn't do you any justice. If people ever look at you in a strange way when having a hypo, just do the sensible thing and ignore them. You do learn something new every day and people who see a diabetic having a hypo will, in fact, learn some interesting information on how to handle any diabetic who is having one.

I never used to wear anything showing that I was diabetic, but it is the most important thing to do. Hypos are a huge worry. If you do have an extremely bad one, and you are about to pass out, anyone who is nearby might check to see if you are carrying anything to identify a problem. If you aren't wearing anything you may get the odd idiot who thinks you're having a sleep or someone who thinks a person has been drinking a lot, and have just passed out. ID bracelets aren't hard to get hold of, it is vital that you get one in case of emergency. I have had many bad hypos, I was stupid for not eating properly before exercise, and I have ended up nearly falling into a coma. Very bad hypos end up with you feeling like you're in a dream - not a wonderful dream where everything is okay, but a dream where a swamp donkey is giving you a kiss under the mistletoe. Never be ashamed of telling your friends about your diabetes, talk them through what they should do if you have a bad hypo, how much sugar they should give you etc. I had a friend of mine once run away from me when I was shopping, I got very abusive, and started shouting things in a disgusting manner. It would have been scary for anyone to have had to deal with that, but it was me not aware of what was going on. My friend didn't understand, and he thought I was just being rude, but luckily I was close to home and managed to get to the kitchen in time for a sugar top up. I explained to him afterwards what had happened, and he understood the whole situation. Educate your friends, and those around you, as it is so important that they know. They could end up saving your life if you ever hit a sticky moment.

# CHAPTER 4 - MANAGING TYPE 1

Learning to manage your diabetes is incredibly important. It is part of your life, and it won't be leaving anytime soon. It's like the annoying friend who always turns up at your house and stays with you for hours on end. In order for your life and diabetes to fit into one, you need to arrange things that suit your chosen lifestyle. When being told that you have diabetes, you start to worry about change and how you will cope with what lies in front of you. I was shocked and indeed scared when I was told. I started to think how it would affect my dream of being a professional athlete; all I wanted when I was 12yrs old was to be the greatest footballer that had ever lived. At the time you are diagnosed with diabetes you do feel like it's the end of the world and there is no way out, but I can assure you that your world isn't caving in, and the more you feel like you're headed on a downward spiral, then this is how you will end up feeling. None of us wants to feel down-beat, so we turn it around and perform a great wrestling manoeuvre - the Twist of Diabetic Fate. We flip our negativity over and gain momentum, and we come out on top with diabetes tapping out on the 1,2 and 3. We control it correctly, then diabetes is submitting, as we are telling our bodies how we want to feel, and feeling distressed, waving around the white flag are not the intentions we have in mind.

Testing your blood glucose levels is so so so so so, yes so important. I can't tell you how important is, as we need to know where our blood sugar levels are at in order for us to control our diabetes. I will be honest with you and say it is an incredibly annoying thing to do, but the way you have to look at it is it's only a few seconds out of your life to stop, test your blood, and see where your blood sugar levels are at. I find it hard as I'm either styling my hair, painting my toe-nails (I can be weird like that) performing the final scene of The Karate Kid, or admiring pictures of the flashiest trainers to take my mind off the day ahead. Anyone interrupting these treasured moments is heading for a masterful performance of my imitation of the Incredible Hulk. The point that I'm trying to make is: it doesn't matter what you're doing, even if it's the greatest thing that puts a smile on your face. Take the time to test your blood sugar levels. It's 15 seconds of your time, and like magic, it's a now you see it, now you don't scenario. I have had many situations where I thought I had the highest blood sugar but it actually ended up being at hypo level. It was lucky I had tested my blood or otherwise I would have left it and ended up damaging my self, and worrying those who were with me. You may have a bad thirst but it doesn't always necessarily mean that your blood sugar levels are reaching the heights of Mount

Everest. You should try and test your blood sugar levels before each meal, before you play sport, before bed (this is always a good way to get your parents, partner, friends out of your hair, especially if they want to tell you off, or tell you a story talking about the latest Wellington boots being the greatest fashion accessory) remember testing your blood is far more important. I try and aim for 6-7 times a day when testing my blood. I am now part of the Diabetic Pump family, and it is extremely important to test your blood sugar levels all the time. If you know in your heart of hearts that you are trying your best to improve your diabetes, then you're on the right track. If you have struggled in the past with testing your blood, then start now, start today, there is no time like the present. Once you get into a set routine, then it will become part of your everyday routine. One test session leads onto 2 test sessions, then leads onto 3, then so-on and so-on. Just so I test my blood, I make sure I fit it into my beauty regime, if I can make the time to style my hair for hours on end, then testing my blood can be fitted in.

Blood sugar glucose machines are now small and easy to carry. When I was first diagnosed the machines they had available were as big as a Hollywood superstar's houses. It was a bit like pulling out a mobile phone the size of a brick, in front of people who had fashionable phones that everyone wanted to be seen with. Treat your blood testing machine like a new I-Phone, make it your fashion accessory, everyone is always showing off their new gadgets, so why not treat your machine like the latest must-have smartphone. You are diabetic, so you have a perfectly good reason to show off the tools that are a part of your life. If you aren't able to get a blood testing machine that is ultra hip, then that's fine, whatever machine you have is part of your life, so explain you're with the vintage old school gadgets. I sometimes use my blood glucose machine from the early 90's. I think it's different, it's a part of me, and those who doubt it, well it doesn't concern them, it's what puts a smile on your face, and this is what it's all about.

Having Diabetes does affect your lifestyle, you would be a few fries short of a Happy Meal if you didn't think that. Just because you have to adjust a few things to your lifestyle, in no certain terms does it mean it's the end of the world. The simple message is that you have to take control of your life. It might be hard, to begin with, but like testing your blood sugar levels, make the most important step, and that's making the first step to turning things to suit your needs, and making them a habitual part of your everyday life. I have had many days where I have become frustrated, and generally annoyed, but it is expected as we have a lot to deal with. In the long-run it is much better for you to eat healthily and to maintain a general well-being about yourself. When you head into late age, I'm sure you would love to be as fit as a young person, but most importantly loving the fact the mirror on the wall is telling you that you are indeed the healthiest, vibrant, energetic one of them all. Make this point factual and not fictional. It can be done, and it's just about having that belief that you can do the right thing and lead the life you want to live. We all have a mental locker stored in our mind, many things rush around in our heads, sometimes very negative things or very positive things. We yet again have a choice in what we want to believe, and what actions we want to follow. Great golfing legend Arnold Palmer used to keep saying the following when he needed to pick himself up to gain positive momentum. You can relate these same lines to your diabetes, keep repeating it as a daily affirmation, and before you know it, you WILL have taken these wise words on-board, being able to make them a part of your everyday life.

IF YOU THINK YOU ARE BEATEN, YOU ARE

IF YOU THINK THAT YOU DARE NOT, YOU DON'T

IF YOU LIKE TO WIN, BUT YOU THINK YOU CAN'T

IT'S ALMOST CERTAIN YOU WON'T


IF YOU THINK YOU'LL LOSE, YOU'VE LOST

FOR OUT IN THE WORLD YOU'LL FIND

SUCCESS BEGINS WITH A FELLOWS WILL

IT'S ALL IN THE STATE OF THE MIND


LIFE'S BATTLES DON'T ALWAYS GO

TO THE STRONGER OR FASTER MAN

BUT SOONER OR LATER THE MAN WHO WINS

IS THE MAN WHO THINKS HE CAN

Doctors will advise all of us that sport and exercise are the greatest ways to help us control our diabetes and to watch our weight. It is cheeky when the doctor can be seen as very lazy, and overweight dishing out this advice, so just tell yourself your own advice; I'm doing this for me, and not for others, as your life is run by you, and not someone who thinks they know your body better than you. The thing is not all of us are sports-people, and some fear the fact they have to get up away from that TV screen from either watching films or playing on their gaming gadget. Exercise is incredibly important, it does help us control our blood sugar, and keep us in the correct blood sugar level range. When I was first diagnosed I can remember that I hated the fact I was told that I couldn't eat sweets, but in some ways, this did save me as I got to escape eating the dreaded family desserts cooked by my relatives. This did give me the most acceptable excuse as for why I couldn't eat the wrongful extravaganza put before my very eyes. I was desperate to eat something sweet when I was first diagnosed, I used to have the sweetest tooth and loved munching on Haribo sweets. I have always luckily enough been a very active person, so I constantly skipped, ran around my house like a lunatic wearing a spider-man outfit, and kicked a football round at every given opportunity. I would then test my blood every half hour to an hour, keeping my fingers crossed that my blood sugar was at a hypo level, just so I could eat sugar, and crave my sugar-fix. This was a very stupid thing to do, as the last thing you ever want is a very bad hypo on your hands. You can hardly enjoy a sweet thing when your shaking, stressed and unattractively sweating trying to get your blood sugar back to a normal level. I didn't understand diabetes fully when I was first diagnosed, so this did seem like a very normal thing to do. My point is that exercise is good for you, and keeps you in shape, and helps motivate your body into staying in one great piece, but sometimes over-doing a good thing can also be very dangerous. Never do exercise to have a hypo, so you can have some sugar. It can prove to be dangerous, as you might be on your own, and all of a sudden without realising you're having a bad hypo, you have blacked out in an unconscious state.

# CHAPTER 5 - LIFE EXPERIENCES

I was never sure what would await me in the world of diabetes, but the experiences we encounter in life stay with us through thick and thin. Diabetes doesn't stop you from doing what you want to do. You are the only one who can stop yourself from progressing. It's mind over matter. One thing I have learned is to never be scared of any situation's outcome. Life is like a yo-yo: up and down. You're never sure just where things are going to end up. It's always best to believe that you will end up on top of the highest mountain rather than stay at the bottom, not willing to take the risk. Pessimistic, negative people have viewed everything I have wanted to do in life as out of my range. I don't live my life for others. They aren't the ones who know what really is going on upstairs in this marvellous mind of mine. You have to live life for you and no one else. You have a dream you chase it. You get a knock back, you get up and go at it again. Diabetes might be able to floor us for a few moments in our lives, but it doesn't control our minds and willpower. Like cream, we rise back to the top. Diabetes might be able to bring us down for a moment but it certainly won't beat us. I have always tried to maintain a strong determination to do what I have wanted to do in life. If it means ignorant people trying to stop me moving forward, then it gives me that extra ounce of energy and power to keep on moving forward in order to bring more happiness into my life. A smile on your face will go a long way as it means people who try and hurt you aren't succeeding. Their words are like olive oil off a Turk's back.

If you have the drive to want to become a sportsperson and you're diabetic, then you really have to take extra care of yourself, as your blood sugar level is more than likely going to head down to dangerous hypo region. Diet is important for all diabetics, but when playing a sport you have to be that extra bit careful. From a young age when I played football, I always made sure of having a good meal before playing. The most important thing was me testing my blood before stepping out onto the playing field.

I eventually turned professional when I was 18 and my dream took me to Turkey. In England many of the pro football clubs I had played with as a youth player knew and understood the effects of diabetes. I remember when playing in a cup football match for my school one summer's afternoon I hadn't eaten my lunch properly and thought I could play a full 90 minutes game without eating a meal and injecting myself with my usual dosage. Oh, how wrong I was.

I remember the second half of the match. My head started spinning and my vision went blurry. (In fact, with the way my vision was I might have found my headmistress attractive when she really resembled the female version of Santa Claus.) I was an idiot and I tried to keep playing. I didn't want to let my teammates down. If I'm honest, though, I also think I was too proud to let people know I was having a hypo. I thought others wouldn't understand and that they would think I was making excuses.

You can't think like that. Never be too proud to let people know you are having a hypo. People are there to help. We can't deal with some situations on our own. Hypos don't allow us to sort it out on our own. If the hypo goes into the danger zone then we need help.

A good friend of mine at school who played on the same team could tell that something wasn't right. I wasn't playing like I usually do - the Ronaldo skills weren't as bobby dazzler as usual - so it was good to see someone noticing something wasn't in order. Luckily for me, he managed to get to the sidelines, get Lucozade for me, and make sure it went into my system in an instant. It was like an awesome magic trick: now you see it now you don't. I was a bit shaken up by this as the effect it had taken on me was very dreamlike. It didn't feel like it was actually happening.

I remember when I was on trial in Turkey that I would have to look after myself better, as diabetes was looked on in a strange way. I felt I would definitely be seen as an outcast, as someone who wasn't capable of playing sport at a higher level. I wasn't going to sit down and take that ignorant chit-chat. The way to prove anyone wrong is to stand tall and do what you do best. Excel at the job you have chosen and your diabetes are pushed to the back of the list. Like anything, if you are great at something it distracts those who have no understanding away from the fact you have diabetes.

On my trial for Turkish first division side Alatay FC, I managed to score a hat-trick whilst turning up the heat on the field of play. I made sure I had eaten well before kick off and my blood sugar levels were at a satisfactory level before I stepped out into the cauldron of fear.

After the trial match, everyone congratulated me, but a few of the players' faces seemed a little bit worried when they saw me testing my blood after the game. This was totally new to them. They had never seen someone who had to test their blood or inject themselves. This didn't bother me: I would educate them about diabetes. Nothing is certain in life; there could be a chance that one of them might later develop diabetes. There are many diabetics worldwide, but in a lot of countries it is seen as a weird curse of nature and diabetics are treated like they are ill and weak. I never got this impression from the other young players. It seemed they were fascinated by the way I dealt with it.

After my first trial, I flew to Istanbul and stayed with a mighty European football club for a couple of weeks to have a trial spell. The club was Galatasaray and - like their nickname "the lions" - they had the passion to play the game like I had the passion to educate people about the mighty force to be reckoned with that is diabetes.

It was an amazing set-up. People were very friendly. The players were down to earth but the coaches, it seemed, were a bit standoffish when they found out I had diabetes. They didn't really understand the whole concept. This made me angry. When you don't ask questions, you never know the answers. I never had any bad hypos whilst I was playing there. The players, like the players at Altay, were intrigued. I guided them through it, and they seemed grateful to learn. Footballers know about muscle tears and ligament damages so why shouldn't they know about diabetes? It can affect anyone.

I eventually signed a professional contract with Altay. I was hoping this was where my football dream would begin. I kept my diabetes quiet to begin with as I didn't want the football coaches or manager to see me as a weak link. On my first day I had to keep sipping Lucozade as I was feeling low and my body was struggling to cope with the heat. The reserve manager kept asking his assistant why I was taking so many breaks. It wasn't like I was sitting down and sticking my feet up! I just needed sugar as I was being put through my paces and I didn't want to flake out on my first day trying to impress.

The training got harder, and the team kitchen was giving food out at lunch with hardly any carbohydrates in it. This went on for a good month or so and I was beginning to struggle. People were looking at me in an odd kind of way. One player who spoke very good English did in some kind of way understand the process of me needing sugar. My Turkish isn't fluent so some of the words I would speak with the non-English players may have been hard for them to understand.

I wanted to explain to the coaches that I had diabetes. I needed someone to understand if I was going to be playing at my very best. It just seemed the older people were very ignorant and didn't want to know. This frustrated me. I felt like telling the oldest coach that, at his age, a walking stick and a wig would be essential if he wanted to fit into the classic old age pensioner gang. There isn't much point in getting on the same level as them; ignorance can breed ignorance, so it is best to not get wound up in situations like this.

One Sunday afternoon when the team was playing at its home stadium, I had injected myself and not eaten any breakfast: I had just had some fruit juice and a slice of bread. I went to the stands with the youth team to watch the game and I was slowly going through a bad hypo stage. My blood sugar was obviously very low but I was trying to ignore it and to just get on with having a bit of banter with the younger kids. I was daft and very stupid. I wasn't taking care of myself. Then it hit me. I went into a very bad state. The sweat was dripping from the brow of my forehead. I was shaking and started to talk like a drunk. Not a lot of sense coming from my mouth. My vision became dreamlike; it didn't seem like it was really happening, but it was. Luckily for me, some of my teammates saw what was happening and remembered what I had I told them: "If I seem weird or funny just feed me sugar." So coke and any sugar substance they could find was being shoved into my mouth at lightspeed, faster than Han Solo's Millennium Falcon from Star Wars.

I eventually came round. I was embarrassed. I had an awful headache and was upset with myself for not letting anyone know about my diabetes. When mistakes are made you learn from them. Life is an experience with all that you come up against. My teammates seemed worried and it was nice to see that most of them wanted to understand and try to help me if it ever occurred again. I went home that night deeply upset. My time in Turkey thus far had been fun but also a struggle. I wasn't going to let this beat me. If you think you are beaten, you are.

Things happen and you don't look back; to move forward you have to look ahead. I went on the following day to train and was a bit worried about what was going to be said about me and my stuntman attack. The coach was standoffish with me and treating me like a child who needed a lollipop to calm him down. The chairman had been told about my attack and he reacted in a very harsh way. He spoke with the most unwise words I had ever heard: "DIABETICS CAN'T PLAY FOOTBALL, THEY CANT HANDLE THE EFFECTS!" My pro contract was terminated. I was told to leave. I didn't have a future with the club.

This hurt immensely. An ignorant football big-wig felt anybody with a health problem wasn't able to play sport at a professional level. Professional athletes such as the great Tottenham Hotspur footballer Gary Mabbut and Olympic gold-medallist Sir Steven Redgrave would have been extremely disappointed by the words that had been spoken to me. These two sporting greats were diabetics. They had been through tough times, but they overcame the odds and rose to the top of their profession. They would not be beaten by diabetes. I admired their spirit and charisma. It was nice to see that I wasn't on my own. Other people had experienced what I had gone through.

It felt like it was me against the world. I wanted to prove a point, but that would have put me on the road to nowhere. When people like my coach and the chairman feel they know it all, they can't hear facts. Ignorance at times like this can be bliss. There was no need to explain me. The explanation isn't necessary for those that believe. I believe that diabetics are able to do anything. If someone feels they can play the role of the head doctor without any medical qualifications, then so be it. I left Altay with a smile on my face, my head held high. I was proud that I picked myself up and vowed to carry on reaching for my goals in life.

I certainly wasn't going to allow some rocking-chair-specialist-middle-aged-man to put a dent in my football career. I ended up going to a team in Ankara called Genclerbirligi. This team were well-known for producing young players and taking them to greater heights, so I felt it was a great chance for me to show off my breathtaking football skills.

From my previous experience with Altay I decided straight away that I would tell the head coach and all involved with the club that I had diabetes. I wasn't going to have another bobbing-for-chips-in-a-deep-fat-fryer experience on the football field or in the football stands again. If I was going to entertain then I would sing in the shower and showboat on the football field.

The nice thing about my new club was that they were professional on and off the field. They wanted me to have a medical just to be sure my health was up to scratch and I was able to endure the physical side of the game. All players have medicals and the same goes for them. It was great to be treated with respect. With respect those who treat you correctly also gain respect. Altay was a first division club but they didn't have the same level of understanding as

Galatasaray or Genclerbiriligi. For me, my new club was the Harrods of football and Altay was the Pound Stretcher. My medical went according to plan; I passed with flying colours, and my diabetes wasn't seen as a problem. The doctor explained the Dos and Don'ts of diabetes to my club, and they accepted the facts. All they were interested in was what I signed to the club for my football skills and not the fact I had diabetes. Diabetes was irrelevant in terms of picking me to play - if it didn't affect my performance then why should it be a problem?

My time at Genclerbirligi was a success. I did have the odd hypo but I was looked after. I was surrounded by people who took time to care and understand. I learned from the bad experience I had at Altay. I wanted to move forwards and not look back. And that's what I did. The chairman who sacked me for having diabetes may have thought he had done the right thing, but he was wrong. Luckily for me, my focus stayed sharp and, because of my strong way of thinking, there was no reason for failure to happen.

I eventually decided to hang up my football boots and take my entertaining ways onto the stage. I had felt football was the right thing for me, but I realized it wasn't. My real love was entertaining people and putting smiles on their faces. I was ready to take my joking and clowning to the stage with big bright lights awaiting me.

Next superstar job on the list: the pop industry.

I had grown up with the entertainment business. My mum and dad were both involved with it. I knew what awaited me: hard work and bossy people, just like those I had experienced in the sports industry. My mum didn't have any problems with letting people know about her diabetes. She always made sure she informed her co-workers about how to handle diabetes and if a hypo was about to take place. I wasn't going to make the same mistake I had made by not letting my bosses know that I had diabetes. If they didn't understand, they were just going to have to take the Jon-Sel diabetic crash course at his school of excellence.

I joined a boy/girl band called Word on the Street in 1999. We were destined for big things, so being in the public eye awaited me yet again. This time around I wasn't willing to perform my drunken hypo antics. The lifestyle was similar to that of playing football in terms of training: early starts, lots of work on fitness, and handling extreme situations under pressure. I really did need to watch what I was eating and be aware of my blood sugar levels.

I had many things on my mind and at times I wasn't as good as I should have been. Testing my blood sugar levels sometimes didn't happen. I was grown up enough to take responsibility for my actions, but, to be honest, if you had stuck me in kindergarten with the 5 year olds I would have been closer to their mindset. Playing with Lego and Star Wars figures would have topped my list.

Rehearsing all the time at an early start took its toll on me. I always aimed to eat a good breakfast but sometimes I just didn't have time. I didn't want my record company bosses to think I was a weak link or a lazy person. Not everyone understands how diabetes affects our bodies. Not looking after ourselves on a 110 percent level will take its toll.

Our very first gig was an outdoor roadshow for the BBC programme Live and Kicking. We were performing alongside Westlife, 5ive and A1. No one has ever spoken about having diabetes in the pop industry in the UK. It was great to be the only one who could open people's minds to the ever growing super force that is diabetes. The performance went very well; it was great to be allowed to act like a nutcase on stage. My blood sugar levels were at a normal level, so my excuse for looking like the number one candidate for Lunatic of the Year was because of my happiness.

As it was our very first performance together, we decided to go out and celebrate. Perhaps my chances of trying to pull Emma Bunton from the Spice Girls were going to take place - Posh and Becks needed to realise it was time to step down from being a couple of the year. I took my evening injection as usual, but I was so excited that I only had a few nibbles to eat. My blood sugar level was fairly low because I had been energetic all day. Not eating wasn't a very clever thing to have done.

The night went very well and was good fun, but towards the end of the evening, as we were about to leave the nightclub, I started acting very strangely. Well, for me, actually, it was considered acting as normal as ever, so people around me couldn't tell that I was in urgent need of a sugar boost. Most people would think sliding down the bannister in a nightclub making monkey noises was extremely strange, but my band members honestly thought it was me doing the usual Jon-Sel "wrongness."

I had been drinking alcohol, but my behaviour was verging on someone who had been drinking all day. Sammy, one of the girls in my band, though I had been taking drugs. She had never witnessed anything like this, and, as my blood sugar was very low, I was closing in on blacking out. The words I was chatting were distorted and didn't make any sense. It wasn't a pretty sight, judging by what I have been told. The girls in my band knew I had diabetes, and luckily Kirsty had a slight understanding of what should be done. I had talked to my bandmates previously about what to do if things didn't seem normal. We stopped off at a service station on the way back to Windsor, where we were staying that night, and the lovely ladies serviced me with Lucozade and Mars Bars. Yes, they overdid it with the sugar intake, but it was better to be safe than sorry.

I remember coming back round. My head seemed to be resting on a plate of egg and beans. Stylish Jon-Sel started the night looking swish and more charming than any prince but ended the evening looking like a messy caveman who only spoke the words "ooooga booga." (I felt ladies would have been impressed with this look.)

It made me realise that eating after you have injected is so important. Your body needs to fuel to keep on going. Without it, all you are going to do is break down. Luckily for me, I had friends to back me up and support me. It goes to show that people who have never witnessed a bad hypo will immediately presume you are either drunk or you have been taking drugs. The behaviour that you show fits into those categories. It is an essential must that you always have sugar on you whether it is a Mars Bar, Lucozade or glucose tablets and an identity card or bracelet stating that you are diabetic. Life is beautiful, but you could be ending it in sooner than expected if you don't take these precautions. It may be boring trying to remember to do these things but they will save your life.

The next day we had a gig for a radio station in Essex. It was great that the ladies in my band were being so motherly to me, "JON-SEL, EAT YOUR FOOD, JON-SEL, CHECK YOUR BLOOD SUGAR, JON-SEL, ARE YOU OK?" It was sweet of them, but it did begin to do my head in. It reminded me to always be careful with my diabetes, I have one amazing mum and I don't need anymore. (At times it did make me feel like an emperor being fed grapes and cheese, though.) I did tell the girls that this is how I felt. They weren't impressed and spanked my behind. I didn't need to be reminded that I was the naughty boy. The backchat calmed down a little bit.

I thought that I would never have another bad hypo after that experience in London, but when you're busy and energetic all the time it takes its toll on your body. On our first major arena pop tour supporting a major UK pop act, Jon-Sel decided it was time to have another entertaining hypo. We had been promoting up and down the country at various radio road shows and we were on our way to Manchester Evening News Arena to support 911. I hadn't been eating the amount I should have been and we had been using up a large amount of energy. Though I was tired, I wasn't on top form with checking my blood sugar.

As we were about to drive into the back of the arena, I started to act strangely. (Nothing new there.) Mark, our tour manager who I always bantered with, though I was just being my usual cheeky self. Eventually, it clicked for him that I was being odd as I started to twitch my head—it was slightly spasming—and I was making random noises. (A farmer, I'm sure, would have been proud of my impressions of his farmyard animals.)

Mark asked me, "JON-SEL, ARE YOU OK?" And I responded with such a pleasant reply, "SHOW ME THE MONEY!" I kept on saying, "SHOW ME THE MONEY FOOLS, SHOW ME THE MONEY!" Mark parked our vehicle around the corner from the arena and shot off to McDonald's. The ladies had been given the job of looking after the chimpanzee Jon-Sel.

The worst thing about waiting for sugar to arrive was that my condition was getting, slowly but surely, worse. Suddenly fans who were waiting outside the stage door of the arena realised that it was our vehicle and started to approach. This isn't good when you have a band member who isn't in the politest of moods.

The windows on our tour vehicle were blacked out—a blessing in disguise—but you wouldn't have been able to block out the sounds I was making. A sly and cunning move then took place: someone threw a towel over my head to disguise the fact I was having a bad hypo. (I think whoever threw the towel over my head got the idea from watching Stephen Spielberg's alien blockbuster ET.) Mark arrived back in time before the fans got the idea that something was going on. A milkshake was passed into my direction and Mark drove off to the safer place where I could generate myself back to superstar status. I drank the milkshake at light speed, ate a doughnut in one easy step, and in time I began to come round. I didn't remember any of it actually happening, it was the usual dreamlike experience. I certainly didn't remember saying

"SHOW ME THE MONEY," but I was impressed with that line.

I learned from this experience that it doesn't matter how busy you are: you must make your health a priority. We can always make excuses. We as individuals are the ones to blame for our own mistakes. I could easily blame my record company for not making enough time for me to check my blood, etc. If you want to be treated like everyone else, then don't use your diabetes as an excuse. This moment made me realise that I had to take more care of myself and had to always take sugar with me for back up. If we had broken down or got stuck in a heavy traffic jam on the motorway, I would have been in serious trouble. There would have been nowhere to go to get sugar. We all would have been in a bad situation. You have to take responsibility for your actions and it is up to you to look after yourself. There isn't always going to be someone there to pick you up when you fall.

I started to get into the habit of checking my blood sugar levels, but I can admit that it wasn't always on a consistent basis. It was because I was sometimes lazy and not bothered, but I pull the strings in my life so it is my choice of how I look after myself. I can't say that I was impressed with the way that I handled some situations, but I was learning how to improve. The rest was totally up to me.

I had never had a bad hypo whilst being on stage. It had happened on the football field and I can remember that being a nasty experience. It was bound to happen at some point. I wasn't being the great diabetic that I should have been. I was loving being in the band, attending showbiz parties, staying out till late, performing everywhere in the UK, but it was taking its toll on my body. You can't burn the candle at both ends. (The same goes for those who don't even have diabetes.) There were many days when we had about 4 gigs in one day, so that meant leaving a gig in London, shooting off up north to somewhere like Sheffield, and then moving on to Bradford. This was tiring. I was eating as much as I should have been. I did lower my insulin intake. But it wasn't good enough. I still wasn't eating as much as I should have been. This, as always, meant I wasn't giving myself enough fuel to go out and perform my very best.

One day we had a strenuous series of events lined up: a television appearance in the morning for Nickelodeon, then a school gig in Surrey, then heading up north to Doncaster, and finally finishing off with a gig at an over 18s venue in Leeds. I always made sure that I ate well first thing in the morning; breakfast is a key ingredient to starting your day off in style. I always found it hard to eat a good lunch as this was when we were either performing or just chilling out. I was only eating snack foods such as a couple of digestives, a glass of milk, and a piece of fruit. There aren't many carbohydrates in these foods and, with the amount of insulin I had been taking, it was important I was able to back it all up. The lunchtime gig was fine, but it was now vital that I had been able to eat a good evening meal to give me the energy to hold out until the very early hours of the morning.

On this particular day, I remember giving myself more insulin than usual as I had highish blood sugar and I wanted to bring it down. This was all very well, but my mind must have been elsewhere, as I had fish and vegetables with some granary bread. This is a brilliant meal and very good for you, but with no carbohydrates, it was not going to be enough to back up the amount of insulin that I had taken. The gig in Doncaster was set for us to be on stage for about half-past eight, so we arrived at the venue a good forty-five minutes before we took to the stage.

I remember feeling quite low before we went on stage but thought nothing of it. I felt I could handle going on stage for twenty minutes even if I was low on my blood sugar. This is something you should never do. Even if you can't check your blood sugar levels and you feel low, don't take a risk and chance it, always take something just to be on the safe side. I wish I had taken my own advice. Halfway through our set, I started to reach the point of no return. I was doing my usual antics on stage when I suddenly decided to run across the back of the stage. As I was running with such determination - reminiscent of Usain Bolt winning Olympic Gold - suddenly I stumbled and fell awkwardly off the stage. I honestly had no idea where I was or what I was doing and it certainly startled my other band members. Yet again I was thankful that our tour manager Mark was at the side of the stage and able to swoop a large bottle of Lucozade my way. I was incredibly lucky to have that support. If it wasn't for me being surrounded by those who were aware of my diabetes, it could have been very costly, as many mistake low blood sugar antics for drunkenness. Whenever I have had bad hypos, I always vow to never get myself in the situation again, but talk is cheap. It's about handling your business with a sensible head in order to not face these types of situations again.

I have always been incredibly lucky to have support when my blood sugar has been low, but if I'm totally honest I have taken it all for granted. There are only so many times you can learn from such dangerous health situations. I made promises to my family that I would take better care of myself, but this would sometimes last for a week or so before I went back into old habits which could have sent me to the nightmare that is HYPOVILLE.

I have had far too many bad hypos. The worst thing you can do is blame yourself. Look at it as a learning curve, but most importantly, you have to get serious about it. I've seen far too many people take their health for granted and then wish that they had looked after themselves better further down the line. My mum is an example of this. I'll talk in more depth about her later in the book.

The problem we face as diabetics are how the general public react when we are suffering from a hypo. The thing is to never be ashamed and to educate those that don't have the understanding of Type 1 Diabetes. I went on tour, travelling the UK performing in *Fame the Musical*, and I always happily tell whomever that I am a Type 1 diabetic. This then leads to me explaining the differences between Type 1 and 2. Many people think that they are exactly the same. This is when it's great as a diabetic, managing to educate those about the difference and what we Type 1 diabetics have to deal with on a daily basis.

When I was doing *Fame* I very rarely had hypos, but when I did I always managed to snog a Mars Bar in a magnificent manner or romance a bottle of Lucozade at light speed.

I only suffered from one really bad hypo on tour and it was, yet again, another scary experience. I had just finished a matinee performance, so I had a 2-hour break to get a quick bite to eat. I needed it to prepare me for the evening performance. I felt low as I left the theatre, but my stupidity kicked into full gear and I decided to hang in there and wait until I found a restaurant. This was particularly stupid, and I think members of The Only Way is Essex would have been sharper at reacting to a situation like this. Never ever, ever wait. If you feel low, get that sugar into your system. Waiting is not clever and it can always be too little too late. I was with two other cast members and they seemed to think I was behaving in my normal childlike daft ways. I started to make animal sounds, my neck started twitching, and I think they thought I was putting on a show. (A show in which I was telling a story about a chimpanzee that escaped from the London Zoo.) I think they began to get a little bit concerned. They knew not all was well. My words were beginning to get slurred. We found an Italian restaurant and, as we walked in, I was walking oddly, and I was coming across as if I was very drunk. The waiters were apparently staring and they seemed concerned about what they had let into their restaurant.

I was told to test my blood sugar, but I was in no fit state. Sweat was dripping profusely from my forehead and I was shaking intensely. One of the cast members realised that I was in need of sugar, and because they knew something wasn't right, the cast members ordered a bottle of coke. I managed to drink it and it brought me back to the land of the living.

I say this yet again: I WAS LUCKY. My stupidity could have got me into so much trouble. It's just not sensible trying to beat a hypo. The hypo will always win. The way to look at it is like seeing a boxer going into a fight against Mike Tyson without any training. If you neglect your sugar, then you will be knocked out without any chance of survival. Don't take any chances, be prepared, have sugar on you, and be the one that sends a hypo running scared.

I don't discuss high blood sugar problems here because they have never really been a problem for me. High blood sugar has obviously made many unwelcome appearances in my life. I have had times when I have had the rage of the incredible hulk. I've been so tired that my head has bobbed in and out of sleep whilst sitting in a coffee shop. I have drunk what seems like a fridge full of water in a short amount of time. The problems that I have faced with low blood sugar can happen if you're a diabetic that struggles to keep his or her blood sugar levels at a reasonable level. The hospital can be a place where you gain a regular spot, and it seems every time you go back the doctors welcome you with open arms and a look of... "AHHH THE DIABETIC." My visits to the hospital have always been in relation to low blood sugar. I have had the same paramedics a couple of times. They always knew it was me when they got the call to head to my neighbourhood. I have had many people think that when a diabetic loses consciousness it's all down to having a hypo. Oh, how wrong they were! A Type 1 can have problems with low blood sugar and high blood sugar. The doctors don't talk imaginary tales when they tell us it is very important to keep our blood sugar levels in a place that doesn't allow them to shoot up to the moon, and then come crashing back down with a huge thump; to suddenly go wandering to the outback in Australia, and then to then head off to an unknown destination leaving your mind in disarray. All you want is to settle down, knowing that you're going to stay in peace and harmony in mind, body, and soul for a long while.

# CHAPTER 6 - MUM AND THE PITY POTTY

My mum got diabetes when she was in her 20s. This was when diabetes was something that didn't have all the wonder insulins and machinery that we have now. The needles were longer than fingernails seen on contestants on a reality dating show. The blood testing strips were complicated. Guessing your actual blood reading was incredibly tricky as you had to match the colour code with the colours on the blood strip case. I looked at it as if I was going into a sunbed shop to pick a tan: the most highly offensive tan colour was equivalent to having a ridiculous blood sugar reading, one of 20 or more. When I was diagnosed, these things were still around. I had to be old-fashioned with drawing up my insulin and making sure no bubbles were in my vial. Luckily I was diagnosed when new things were breaking through. My mum wasn't as lucky. Doctors were still trying to figure out the best ways to treat Type 1. The dangers of mismanaging your diabetes weren't really discussed in great detail. They knew problems would arise but there wasn't much information on looking at the complications in depth. It's easy to take things for granted.

We all think we are invincible, but what we don't realise is that things can easily catch up with us. There is no escaping the dreaded complications we will encounter if we don't make the effort to look after ourselves. It's only since I attended the Dose Adjustment For Normal Eating (DAFNE) course that I realised how important it is to take great care of ourselves. It is important to take care of yourself if you're not a Type 1 diabetic, but even more so when you're on that mission to provide yourself with good-looking blood sugar readings. A lot of people think all diabetics will live short lives. (The complications that can result from mistreating diabetes are something more horrendous than Louis Walsh serenading you with a rap, dressed in an outfit last seen on the tooth fairy.) The complications need to be taken seriously. It is scary when you hear about the problems that we could face. It isn't a definite fact that we will face these problems; it's a warning that things can go horribly wrong if care isn't taken. We often hear about heart disease, amputations, and blindness. These things can happen if we decide to keep walking down the diabetic highway to uncontrolled diabetes hell. These are just a few of the problems that we could face, but there are other things which could put a dent in our wealth and our health.

I always used to have a polite word in my mum's ear, doing the annoying thing of asking,

"SHOULD YOU BE EATING THAT? HOW MUCH SUGAR ARE YOU HAVING? HAVE YOU HAD YOUR INSULIN? HAVE YOU EVER THOUGHT ABOUT DOING ANY EXERCISE TODAY?" I sounded like a know-it-all, a diabetic who was on top of his game. This was so far from the truth. I just knew that my mum should be taking better care of herself.

Whenever a diabetic is told to do something, we usually end up saying, "YEAH YEAH YEAH, WAIT A MIN, I'M JUST HAVING A TREMENDOUS YAWN." I know I hate it when non-diabetics tend to send information my way which consists of useless facts, and no actual understanding of what we live with. It was hard for me. When you see someone that you love going through hard times, not looking after themselves in the best way possible, then you start to worry about what the future holds. My dad does exactly the same with me, often saying, "JON-SEL, HAVE YOU EATEN? JON-SEL, ARE YOU HAVING A HYPO?" My response always quick-witted, basically translating into, "LALALALALALA I AM NOT LISTENING TO YOU, I KNOW WHAT I'M DOING." So many times I've suddenly passed out, a hypo greeting me with open arms, and I come back round having to swallow my pride. " DAD YOU WERE INDEED RIGHT, I JUST FELT THE NEED TO THROW MY TOYS OUT OF MY PRAM."

My mum knew deep down that she wasn't looking after herself correctly, but we so often don't realise that problems begin to catch you up later on in life if you haven't done the regular things of trying to maintain a healthy lifestyle.

My mum was an actor working hard in the West End when she was first diagnosed. This meant she was always active. She danced, sang and acted 6 times a week, and always did things which helped keep blood sugar levels at a respectable level. My mum was working all the time and always did her injections. She never missed them. But she wasn't testing her blood sugar levels nearly as much as she should have. These factors weren't looked at closely at that time. Now they are discussed at length and taken seriously when you are first diagnosed. We were told that carbs were the main basis of our diet, no sugar at all. Stay away from anything which doctors felt were a no-no to a diabetic's life. Fast-forward a few years and now there is more flexibility with what we eat. Obviously, a healthy diet is what we should aim for but if we have a cheat day, so be it. Don't beat yourself up. (Just be sure to back yourself up with insulin if you have a day where the kid from the Haribo factory decides to tell you to open your mouth so he can throw Tangfastics at a rapid speed into the big hole that is your mouth!) Testing blood sugar is also so important when these small problems happen. It's a minute of your life to check; it's not an eternity. It is going to help you in the long run to address these problems and to get yourself back on that horse heading into a glamorous sunset. You always hear about problems that can overtake us and decide to take a zombie effect on us, so that we resemble cast members of the diabetic walking dead. I used to think it was all rubbish. I went back to the invincible mentality: strength of a thousand lions, eyesight crystal clear, and feet like an Olympian on the running track. This was all going to be proven wrong, as the small troubles I began to face were not on the level of what my Mum was about to go through.

My Mum's lifestyle began to change immensely when she decided to take a back seat to the world of entertainment. In life attitudes can change, choices lead you in different directions. You end up having moments where you feel it is you against the world. I think my mum felt that she didn't need to be as active any more. Exercise is so important, no matter what. It doesn't have to be a process where you're in the gym for a solid 2 hours. It is just important to get your Kim Kardashian booty off a sofa, move, and get that body functioning. A 10 min walk is better than no walking at all. Laziness exists in all aspects of life. We can blame others, but it is very rare that we take note and actually say, "YES, I HAVE BEEN AN ABSOLUTE NUMPTY, I'M RESPONSIBLE FOR MY ACTIONS, AND IT'S TIME I PUT SOME ACTION BACK INTO THIS PITY POTTY ENGINE."

My mum would go to work, she would do the housework, she wouldn't be stuck to a sofa, but more than often she didn't do enough compared to the active lifestyle she used to lead. I think having to worry about testing your blood, watching what you eat so intensely, and remembering to take your injections will have an impact in your life whether you like it or not.

I have been lucky enough in my 28 years of being a diabetic to have not had any severe issues come at me like a Miley Cyrus wrecking ball.

I did have a massive scare a few years ago when my left eye suddenly went bloodshot. There was no pain. I then did the classic self-testing trick of trying to read with the bloodshot eye from distance, and then compared it to the eye that hadn't gone slightly wonky donkey. Fear began to creep in, as my eyesight had always been nearly perfect. It dawned on me that not going for regular diabetic eye check-ups was a stupid thing. Problems can be detected early on. Doctor's appointments are a severe pain if you feel your body is feeling and looking like a

Greek god or Amazonian princess, but it is so important to do the basics. That's going to your regular check-ups throughout the year. My vanity and stupidity were the main cause of this, so in a frenzied rush, I decided to visit the local opticians to see if it was just my vision slowly shifting to the eyesight of an old person who was in need of bling glasses to do a Sudoku puzzle.

The optician put my bruised and battered eye through some intense tests. In situations like this, my bullshit wasn't going to save me.
"Read the letters, Mr Gourkan?"
"Errrrr, Z, X, U, I, O."
"Ahhhh. 2 out of 5 correct."
"Surely many people get that letter line wrong?"
"Well, Mr Gourkan, you will be surprised that many people get at least 4 out of 5"
"NOOOOOOOOOOOOOO."

The dodgy eyeball could have been the main reason why I began to misplace a celery stick for a straw. I was worried. I was scared. It became clear that this was all down to my diabetes being so poorly controlled over the past few years. I had been having intense hypos. I wasn't testing my blood sugar at the appropriate time. My levels were swinging up and down like a hyperactive chimp in the Jungle Book. The optician explained everything, and it was indeed a problem developed through badly controlled diabetes. But the problem had been captured early like a Bear Grylls supper on an island. It could be sorted.

The hospital came next, and the slow process of getting my vision back to the status of a valued member of the X-Men began. I had a tiny leak behind my eye. It is something known as a Macula Odema, something very common in diabetics. Luckily, it wasn't at the stage where I would need laser corrective surgery to sort it, it was a matter of the correct antibiotic, and the most important thing was to start controlling my blood sugars like an A-list celeb on a Hollywood red carpet.

Controlling your blood sugar is so important. My eye doctor emphasized the importance of this. Better control can only help any problem you may face with your eyesight. I booked the DAFNE course straight away. I talked to people who could help me get better control and find a way of getting on the pump.

Months later, the pump was a part of my life, and blood sugars had improved immensely. I started to test my blood sugars at all the appropriate times. Once I had sorted my life and began to understand better the effects diabetes can have on my body, I put myself in a confident place of focusing more on myself. I didn't want later in life to be in the situation of having long-lasting problems that would wreak havoc. My eye got better, the leak stopped, and vision was in a place where I wasn't having conversations with fruit and veg in the supermarket, mistaking a cucumber for a marathon runner. I don't want any diabetic to go through a harsh scare at any point in his or her life. The scare that I had made me buck up my ideas, but sometimes luck isn't always on our side. I would never want anyone to take a risk by not looking after themselves and it is too little, too late.

The problem that I faced was scary, but it was a very real part of what we face as diabetics. My mum, however, hasn't been as lucky, and, as much as it breaks my heart talking about it, it serves as a reminder of how important it is to make the effort, and to take care of yourself.

We can all joke about worst possible outcomes, but, truth be known, it does and it can happen. If complications hit you like a hurricane whipping you up into a frenzied storm, then you have to take stock of yourself and do all that you can to get yourself in a place where you make small improvements.

My mum has been struck with a diabetic take-no-prisoners sandstorm. Her body is breaking down. Problems that could have been prevented have grown so large that they are preventing her from living a life that is meant to be full of joy. You simply can't outrun diabetes when it tries to catch up with you. You will run out of breath. Wherever you go, a small problem is trying to attach itself to you, a problem that will develop into a larger than life Loch Ness Monster persona. My mum is still, to this day, a fighter, and refuses to be beaten, but she tells me all the time: "PLEASE LOOK AFTER YOURSELF. LOOK WHAT DIABETES HAS DONE TO ME." My mum has problems with her heart. She has cardiovascular disease. She had an amputation of one of her toes. She has neuropathy problems; she can't feel any sensations in her feet. She is close to being partially sighted. Alongside these problems, she has been battling lung cancer. She says the diabetic problems have been worse than the fight with The Big C. This is real talk, and seeing my mum battle the complications that have developed as a result of her ignoring her diabetes has proven to me that diabetes is indeed something that needs to be taken seriously.

The doctors can't force you to look after yourself. All they can do is advise and tell you about what could happen if you don't take your diabetes seriously. My Mum is a perfect example of how things can go if you don't treat your diabetes correctly. Seeing what it has done to her is just a small reminder of how one day you can have your health, and the next it has done a Harry Potter disappearance trick leaving you stuck in a pit of despair around the back of Hogwarts. Any of these problems can be avoided. It is down to you being responsible for your own actions and learning to be smart. Pointing the finger at others when your body is breaking down isn't going to turn back the clock and give you health covered in glitter serenading you with colours of the rainbow.

Whenever I have a bad day, or bad times with controlling my blood sugar, or looking after myself in an unsensible manner, I just make myself aware, and realise I am grateful for my current state of health, and that diabetes really isn't going to be something which is going to suck the enjoyment out of life for me. It is horrendous, it is a pain, but so are so many other things in life, there are worse things to be facing, and its just brilliant that we have medication that can help us live a life of glamour and glory. My mum is the reason why I have begun to buck my ideas up. I don't want to feel helpless. Listening to those in the know about diabetes is really important. Yes, some will bore us with their yawn-factor facts, but beneath the boredom, there is real talk. Those words can help protect us even more so if we are willing to make even the smallest of changes to our everyday life.

Be smart, don't overanalyse. Focus on you, invest in you, and learn from your mistakes. Never beat yourself up. If you do, you knock yourself out of ever rising up and conquering again. Life is to be lived. Have the intelligence to amend your ways if you ever feel you're sliding down a slippery slope. As long as you're alive, you will always have a chance of making it. Never admit defeat. Have those doctors in your diabetic clinic staring at your wonderful stats, and just say to yourself, "My life, My rules, My diabetes."

I have always been strong enough to take whatever diabetes threw at me on the chin. Surprisingly enough my chin has taken a lot of hits but thankfully it has got more staying power than Robbie Rotten's from Lazy Town. It is expected that we will all have times when we feel down and defeated, but I never felt I would allow diabetes to take me into a dark place where I began to feel sorry for myself. In my younger days, I was fearless. I felt invincible with a strength so powerful that I could overturn the odds at the drop of a hat. I felt a sense of guilt when I began to really start feeling sorry for myself. The pity potty seemed to become a place that I wanted to stay attached to as long as the entirety of Game of Thrones. The very bad hypo that I suffered from - and very nearly knocked on the doors of heaven and hell - had put me in a state of worry, a state of a quick realisation that diabetes can't be taken with a pinch of discount value salt.

When bad times arise in a diabetics life, we have what seems like a stadium full of people criticising and passing off their opinions on how we should handle our life. Friends and family all concerned, and all piping up with views we have heard before. A lecture which seems to go on and on and on and on, the yawn effect taking place and all we want is to stick some earplugs in and nod our heads at the words firing out in our direction. I always say to my dad, who is my number one fan and one who worries constantly about me living with diabetes, that unless you have it then you will never know what we go through. This is just me reacting with rage and anger, as deep down his words are indeed true. It's me running from the truth. No one likes to admit that they are in the wrong.

We live with diabetes and we face many stupid remarks from a lot of people. Those who really have no clue are looking for an opportunity to vent their own frustration and aim it in our direction. It doesn't matter what small minds think about the way we live our lives; those who aren't willing to learn will eventually get stuck in situations where they feel a carrier bag from a supermarket would make good use as a parachute when jumping out of a plane. Small words from irrelevant people wind me up the most, and my family adding concern to my welfare also adds a pinch of rage, but they are two different types of wind up. The ones who care do it for a valid reason. The others do it as their opinions aren't accepted in real life; hence why they pipe up, becoming trolls with very unattractive personalities.

The hypo I had which very nearly put a stop to my waltzing in life really shook me up. This happened 28 years after I was diagnosed. I had never let anything put me in a state where I would feel sorry for myself. This time it was totally different, and it was a wake-up call, a wake-up call far worse than farmyard animals making enigmatic noises in my precious earhole. I have never felt sorry for myself in regards to my diabetes, and I always felt I could be the one to help advise others when dealing with it, but this time around I felt alone as if no one would be willing to listen. The majority of people pass judgement without knowing the truth. 28 years on and I had had enough of living with diabetes, enough of everything involved with dealing with it. I just didn't understand why I was having to deal with it, and I started asking stupid questions like, "WHY ME? WHY DID I GET IT SO YOUNG? WHAT DID I DO TO DESERVE IT?" People usually ask these questions when they're first diagnosed, but I was asking 28 years later.

A few days after hitting an all-time low, and taking on board everything my dad had told me, I just wanted to shy away from everything and behave like I didn't have diabetes. My head was down, and I was in a situation where I was wallowing in my self-pity. I felt like I had no way of getting out, and I was going to be stuck in a dark gloomy hole for the rest of my life. I was being an idiot. The more I felt sorry for myself, the more horrendous I would feel, and this was certainly raising hell with my blood sugar levels. If I have had hard times with my diabetes, one thing I have never done is miss out on giving myself my insulin. Stress causes all types of problems for a diabetic, and as always everyone is different, so depending on the person, blood sugar levels react differently to certain situations. My blood sugar levels were starting to be happy staying sky-high, and my face was slowly but surely turning into a miserable grump on the level of the Grinch. I didn't want to face the world, and even though people wanted to help, they just started giving medical advice which made them feel like they were on the verge of getting a miracle cure for treating diabetes. They say Time is a great healer, but I wasn't helping myself to try and rise back up to put a smile on my face again. The more I wallowed, and began to stay stuck on my little pity potty, the worse I got due to my diabetes not getting the tender loving care that it needed.

When you don't look after your diabetes, you start to gain a weary head which starts to fill up with lots of unwanted voices telling you to give up, to just admit defeat. We all fight battles, and sometimes other worries will overtake us dealing with our diabetes. The thing to do is to BREATHE deep, sit on your own, and calm yourself down. I am the last person to take this kind of advice, seeing as I'm always so manic, and calm is a swear word in the world of Jon-Sel. If we build all our stress up by adding more pointless things to the situation, then it's obvious that we are just going to feel like we are on a sinking ship, with no chance of anyone coming to save us.

It took me time to snap out of my grump, but I look back at it now and realise just how stupid I had been. I was being so hard on myself. I had got to the stage where I had to look back at how I had handled my diabetes previously. I had survived, I had smiled, and I was turning my diabetes into a bigger problem, but all because a shock to my system had made me overanalyse how I had been living my life.

Beating yourself up gets you nowhere. It leaves you stuck in the mud. In life, if you want to move forward, you have to stop looking behind. Put all importance on focusing on the now. I have taken far too many things for granted. Imagine if you had been a diabetic in the 1970's? The medication wasn't like it is now. It was like a death sentence. I am grateful that I never encountered that situation. Everything has advanced, and diabetics' lives have been made easier with the treatments we now have at our fingertips.

We are all different. We will all handle things differently. But the best advice I can give is to not be hard on yourself. Not everyone will understand. The main thing is that you understand what you have to deal with and to take each day as it comes when looking for ways that are going to help you deal with living with diabetes. I am not going to lie - I still have days when I am fed up, and start getting upset with the word diabetes, and the measuring of the carbs I am about to eat. I will usually dust myself off, look in the mirror, and say, "TOMORROW IS A NEW DAY; WE GO AGAIN."

Never compare yourself to others who have diabetes. Like I keep saying, we are all different, and we run our own race when dealing with it. Some Type 1's are amazing, and they always have amazing HBAC1's, but this doesn't mean you are an awful diabetic if your results haven't been at the near perfect level. We all have our own vision of how we want to live our life. It is down to you to live the life that you have set out for yourself. My HBAC1 has indeed got better, but I have had some awful results. My success has been down to a variety things which have been affecting me in life. The diabetic pump for one has helped me gain better control, but some diabetics have better control taking Novorapid and Lantus injections. Focus on your results, and your diabetes, as it is your body which needs to be looked after. Others' diabetic results have no relevance in your life whatsoever. It is easy to look at others and pass judgement, but it isn't going to get you closer to walking the red carpet in Hollywood; allowing that judgement to affect you is worrying about things that aren't going to help you conquer the road to gaining main event diabetic supremacy control at Wrestlemania.

# CHAPTER 7 - LIFE ON THE PUMP

When I was first diagnosed with diabetes, the diabetic pump was something that we would all dream about in terms of making our lives easier when trying to control it. I never thought something so amazing as the pump would ever exist in my lifetime. I just thought that huge syringes would become my best friend, and having to stay away from anything sweet would be something I would have to forever live with. Times have definitely changed, and it seems we are always lucky enough to have new things sent our way in order to make our lives easier. The pump has apparently been available for a long time, but I wasn't told about it for many years later, and it seems that there are loads of diabetics who are kept in the dark about things which can help their control reach a sensible level. I was lucky enough to have come across a younger diabetic who told me about it, and told me how it has changed her life for the better. When you hear news like this coming from a fellow diabetic, it would be stupid not to listen, and to see if it would help how you control your diabetes. It seemed that the doctors that I had bumped into weren't very helpful when asking about the facts of a diabetic pump, and how I would be able to go about getting one.

It's always very hard, and it can put a downer on things when you try to confide in your doctor, and they don't want to help you resolve your current situation to put you in a much better place. Unless you are a diabetic, then you won't understand how our blood sugar levels being all over the shop, can put us in moods which would put the incredible hulk to shame, and would even scare off an army trying to bring down the Avengers once they had assembled. It would be sensible for those with the power to help to actually take note and always try to put any new information they have heard out our way. It takes a few seconds, and as diabetics, we are entitled to get the information which could well indeed put us in better situations with how we live our lives.

Once I had done my research on the pump, I was a bit sceptical about carrying around a little device which I felt may annoy me, as it would always be attached to me. In these kinds of situations, you have to weigh up the pro's and con's; "How will it work for me? Will I benefit from using it? Will it suit my lifestyle? Will my diabetes be more improved? Will I be happier and feel better?" You have to sit down and write all these questions down, ask your diabetic consultants, ask close friends.  You are never alone and your diabetic consultants are there working for you, they want to help you.

Speaking from my own experiences, I would have to say that I have never found my local doctors helpful with these situations, so I always pushed forward, and hassled my consultants who worked in the diabetic units.  As a diabetic, you are always entitled to get advice, and to get help with the problems you face. The one thing which can annoy a lot of diabetics in the U.K. is the months course that you have to go on in order to be considered for a pump.  The thought of being told about diabetes and the problems we face, and how we can treat it better, is my idea of living in reality TV hell.  It would be like being on a stage with a puppet nagging on in a ridiculous voice on a Britain's or America's Got Talent stage, constantly being told:  "DON'T DO THIS, DON'T DO THAT".  I was being a stubborn little know it all.   We always have room to learn, but the fact that I had been a diabetic for over 25 years meant I didn't want to be told how to live with it.  It was so far from the truth as these DAFNE courses are nothing like that whatsoever.  Feeding your mind with new knowledge, refreshing your brain with new information is the best way to go about business, you learn something new, then it's down to you putting it to good use, and perhaps helping yourself live a happier healthier life.  The best thing about the months course is the fact you get to meet another type 1's, this helps others as sometimes we think we are the only ones who deal with it.

You learn a lot about how diabetes really works, and how it can affect your body in the long term, and the biggest bonus is the free food you receive, and gadgets from companies such as Accu-chek, and Medtronic.  The reason why it's recommended you go on a course like this is to help you with carbohydrate counting, and this is important if you're going to go on a pump as this is how you monitor everything.   Even if you feel that a pump isn't right for you, it's still great, and so important to have the carb counting understood, as it will help when working out your doses when injecting at meal and snack times.  My diabetes has improved so much since I went on a pump, but it hasn't always been plain sailing.  I have done many stupid things, as I have gone about my business by thinking I could do things my way, and when you have a mentality like that, it ends in tears and can put an end to your life.  I hate using words which talk so negatively, but the truth needs to be told as it can help save someone's life if they have made the same mistakes I have made.

If problems ever arise with your pump, and you feel the correct dose of insulin isn't being delivered or too much is being given, then always be sensible and consult your diabetic nurse/consultant. It is their job to help you, and there is no shame in asking for help. The main problem that I deal with is low blood sugar. I have the worst fear of getting high blood sugar. I am so obsessed with keeping my blood sugar levels at such a low level, that it had been putting me in such a bad place in terms of sending me to Hypoville (HYPO). I started to not put my trust in my pump, and thinking I was invincible I felt that I could just happily give myself little doses of insulin without consulting my blood sugar machine first. This is such a bad thing to do, it's like jumping into the sea with high winds coming in from all angles and expecting to stay afloat. The hypos I was beginning to receive were similar to the Titanic sinking, except I was lucky enough to rise back up with the help of glucose tablet armbands.

In 2016 I came close to going into a diabetic coma, and this was all down to my stupidity in not wanting to get high blood sugar. I was out celebrating my birthday and I had been eating a lot of food which contained the entire sugar content of Willy Wonka's chocolate factory, and I was also drinking alcohol which does indeed wreak havoc with one's blood sugar levels. I had tested my blood sugar levels before I had my meal which was a heavenly mix of carbohydrates full of absolute junk. I had given myself the correct amount of insulin needed and even increased the carb amount by a little bit. I was being extra careful as I knew my blood sugar levels would be dancing into the danger zone in a few hours time. The evening was going well; I was having fun and busting out moves that belonged in Vegas alongside Britney Spears when the clubs were closed. Every time I had a drink which contained a lot of sugar or wasn't on a diet level, I would go to my pump and just give myself more insulin. I was at the stage where I couldn't bother to test my blood, it was me being lazy, and also thinking that I knew it all and didn't need to abide by the rules by checking my blood sugar levels. Alcohol can make you feel like you have high blood sugar; the thirst has you slurping, and you're so dehydrated that it's like you're in the Sahara desert looking for an imaginary water fountain sprouting out of the sand. I was actually believing I had mystical powers where I could imagine my exact blood sugar level by not actually testing it. In my 28 years of being a diabetic, I did the stupidest thing that I had ever done, and that was to give myself around 8 units of Novorapid without checking my actual blood sugar levels. I felt that if I was going to continue to drink, then the amount of insulin I was going to give myself was going to cover me. I am lucky to be alive to tell this story, but I was such a stupid boy, and so dumb that I was making someone dressed as a chicken who goes on the X-Factor seem more intelligent. The drunker I got, the more I wasn't going to be able to get any symptoms from suffering from a hypo. It had reached the stage where my blood sugar levels were dropping at a drastic rate, and I was totally unaware of what was going on. I was too drunk and had probably been suffering from a hypo for a good 15 mins before I left, where I had been behaving like a child riding a giraffe from Toys 'R' Us. I can only recall tiny segments of the night, but I remember leaving in my drunken haze, and starting my walk home.

That's where it ends, I remember nothing after that, apart from when I woke up in the back of an ambulance attached to a Glucose IV. I had no idea what was happening, but thankfully I had been saved in the nick of time. The paramedic was as smooth as you like, he was speaking to me like I was a customer in the Queen Vic in Eastenders. "Jon???? Can you hear me matey????" My head was wobbling around like an excited bobblehead, and I sounded like I had crept out of a swamp with goo dripping from my mouth. The fact I was alive should have been my main reason to have been so happy, but I was actually so angry that the paramedic was getting my name wrong. In my hypo haze as I was coming back around, I kept saying "It's JON-SEL", "Yes Johnny" the paramedic replied. For the first time in a long while, I didn't react, and just said to him "THANKS SO MUCH". He gave me a sly nod and just said no worries mate. I began to ask him what had happened? where did I end up? It seems not all human beings is interested in just themselves, I was lucky enough to have had a couple of people pass me when I was out for the count at 3 am. Apparently, I had been found in a ditch alongside the main road, and the reason they had reacted in calling 999, was that they thought I was having a heart-attack.

Everyone reacts differently when having a very bad hypo, I happen to twitch and move around like a breakdancer busting out a turtle move. They were concerned as it's not often you see a young man in a ditch passed out and making odd sounds. I was so lucky to be alive, and if they hadn't had called emergency services then I would have ended up in a diabetic coma, become brain dead, and wouldn't be alive to be able to tell this story now. Not everyone is as lucky as this, I could have passed out in the middle of the road, and been ran over, I could have been left alone with no-one to attend to my needs, and ended up never coming back around. I never use to wear a diabetic alert band, but it seemed this also helped my cause this time around. The bright pink bracelet wrapped around my wrist stands out like fake tan on an incredibly pale person. This is why wearing alert bands are so important, it helps notify those who don't know what illness you are suffering from.

Luck had indeed worked in my favour, but it began to sink in that more care was going to be needed for dealing with my diabetes. The paramedic told me that my blood sugar level would have been around 1.2 when I passed out, and as I was attached to my glucose drip my blood sugar levels were coming round to about 3.6, slowly but surely getting me back into a safer place again. The experience I went through that evening was the worst I had ever been faced with in the 28 years that I have been a diabetic. It proves that you need to always wear a medical id tag, always carry glucose or sugar on you, and never guess blood sugar levels before giving yourself your insulin. I was angered at myself for my stupid actions, but one thing you should never ever do is beat yourself up about the way you dealt with a situation, that you didn't do things by the diabetic guidelines. You're only human, and mistakes as always will be made.

The thing to do is to learn from these mistakes, ask for any help from those at your diabetic clinic, and to move on with your head held high at all times. It took me a while after this incident to deal with what had happened, it bucked up my ideas as I was so close to losing my life. We often take many things for granted, but with your health, you have to be so on top of your game and especially if you have diabetes.

My diabetes has been better in the long-run since I began life on the pump. Mistakes will always be made, but the best way of dealing with these situations is to learn from all the problems you face. I highly recommend the pump to all Type 1's, but not everyone will have the same outlook on how they wish to treat their diabetes. When I attended the DAFNE course, the main aim was to learn new things and to get myself on the pump. The guys I did the course with were a lot older, and also a lot younger, but a few of them felt life on injections was better than being attached to a pump.

I felt exactly the same way when I first found out about it, my ideas behind it were like I would be attached to a clamp, and lugging around something that I would have pay a massive amount of money for if getting it onboard a plane. The best advice I can give is to always do research, look into things, and see if they could help make your life easier. You don't have to agree to anything that you aren't interested in; it's your body, and as always you pull the strings on how you want to live your life. Don't ever be pushed into something that you feel won't work for you. The consultants that deal with you looking after your diabetes will always want the best for you. If you don't agree with something, then don't shy away, you are already courageous enough having to deal with type one, so speak your mind, and don't be pushed into anything that you feel won't work for you.

There will always be pros and cons to any type of diabetic injection. I do sometimes miss the normal injection procedure, as I feel like I'm carrying around a newborn baby, and having to look after him/her with such care. I go to the toilet, and I suddenly forget I'm attached to Melvin the Accu-chek pump child and it just drops down from my waist, and I have a little outburst featuring swear words which aren't really spellbinding.

I also have the odd small problem when sleeping at night, and as I roll over it is rubbing into my groin and this has just disturbed my sleep, which had me doing the salsa with Cinderella on top of a pumpkin. These are small nuisances, I can live with them as they annoy me for 3 secs of my life. That is nothing if in the long-run my blood sugar levels are nearing perfection, and my mood swings aren't all over the place.

The pump has changed my life, and all for the better. My stupidity didn't allow me to get on it sooner; I built ideas up in my head which were actually non-existent, and so far from the truth. Treat it as your best friend, and when you click you will know that this is something that is only going to build you into a healthier better version of your current self. The Novorapid flex pen was my best friend for many years, but he kept leaking in my pocket, and I had to head off into the diabetic clinic sunset, and book a meeting with my relationship counsellor DAFNE, and from that moment on I was introduced to my pump buddy. 4 years on, we are closer than ever, but we do have the odd tantrum due to me being naughty and not showing Melvin the care that he deserves.

Do the right thing today, and go and find out if there is a chance of moving on to some new diabetic wonder technology. Ask for information, get yourself involved, and most importantly do what makes you the happiest, and never feel awkward if you want to try a new way of treating your diabetes. The pump may not be for you, but if you haven't been on the DAFNE course, then do yourself a favour and book yourself in right away. Learning is key, and knowing all the facts is only going to help you in the long run.

# CONCLUSION - NEVER DEFEATED

I have always felt that it was me against the world with Type 1 diabetes. I have met many Type 1's and a fair few Type 2's, and it seems that whatever type you have been diagnosed with that you will meet many people that just don't understand how deadly this illness is. Type 1 and 2 are different, yet the outcome of both, if treated badly, is severe and extremely dangerous. A step in the right direction would be for the Press to educate the general public, to communicate that Type 1 isn't down to someone eating junk food consistently. The moment this is all cleared up, and improvements are made to raise awareness in the correct manner, then perhaps we will be a little bit closer to a Type 1 diabetic being accepted for who they are.

I know full well that I'll still get comments hurled my way.

"YOU EAT TOO MUCH"
"YOU'RE NOT LIKE AUGUSTUS GLOOP"
"WERE YOU BORN IN A DRIVE THRU????"

The problem is, when an 8-year-old child states that they are diabetic, they are thin, they are healthy, and an adult with no education decides to pipe up, "OI LITTLE ONE, YOU AIN'T A DIABETIC, YOU'RE SKINNY, YOUR DOC'S LYING TO YOU, YOU'RE A LYING ATTENTION SEEKING SHIT." This kind of behaviour exists. I have endured it throughout my diabetic life. 13 years old and being told to not inject in front of people in a restaurant. I always knew how to stand up for myself. "NO, I WON'T, I AM A DIABETIC, I HAVE TO DO THIS, YOU DON'T LIKE IT THEN DON'T WATCH, IF I DON'T DO IT, THEN I DIE."

Not all young Type 1's, nor all older Type 1's stand up for themselves. This is why I feel the need to explain what has happened to me. It has been tough, it has been rough. I never had a Kate Winslet to give me a cuddle when on a sinking ship in what we call life. I have taken the knocks, and I have seen first hand the ignorance around diabetes. I do feel for Type 2 diabetics. But I feel more for Type 1's as that's what I fight on a daily basis. We all fight battles that no one knows anything about, but the important thing is to educate: open people's minds, share experiences, and a majority of mine seem that I could have ended up in an asylum, but "IT WAS JUST A HYPO DEAR." The moment I don't see a headline in a magazine or newspaper stating

"EAT FRUIT AND CURE DIABETES, STICK A CHEERIO AROUND YOUR WAIST TO STOP DIABETES, CURE DIABETES BY WALKING LIKE AN EGYPTIAN....JUST STATE ITS TYPE 2 YOU'RE TALKING ABOUT."

We need people to know the truth. Social media has endless rants about it. Unfortunately, those with the power to change things never like to admit that they are in the wrong. I will keep being strong. I will keep raising awareness. Not everyone will understand my way of putting things across, but why change being who you are when talking about something that you are so passionate about.

I hope there will be a day when a cure appears, and all diabetics can tell a beautiful story of "ONCE UPON A TIME, I HAD DIABETES." I am not a perfect diabetic. I try my best. Life is to be lived, but the most important thing is to do it sensibly. The worst thing is ending up with blindness, an amputated limb, a body that can't move. You want to smile, so don't think you know better than everyone else. Ask for help. I am my own worst enemy. and luck won't always be on your side when diabetes is involved.

WE CAN LIVE WITH IT, WE CAN BE HAPPY, WE CAN BEAT IT. The more you keep up with things, the more you will conquer the word itself, diabetes, which many people just want to divorce immediately.

Dust yourself off, raise that head up high, shout out a tremendous WOOOOOOOOO, and when needs be, you just wink and tell the world in victorious voice: "DIABETES WON'T DEFEAT US!"

Printed in Great Britain
by Amazon